Scarred

Proof of Survival, Marks of Strength

Dr. Ivon L. Valerie

SAPIENTIAL | WE
PUBLISHING | PUBLISH
THE WISE

Sapiential Publishing

CONTENTS

DEDICATION

This book is dedicated to every soul who has felt the weight of past wounds pressing on their heart. May these pages shine a light on your path, remind you of your worth, and guide you toward the proper healing and purpose God has intended for you.

Acknowledgements

I thank God for the grace to speak into deep places of pain. I appreciate those who courageously shared their stories with the world. You're showing that healing is real and hope is not far away. I honor every counselor, pastor, mentor, and friend who stands as tall support pillars when trauma seems overwhelming. Lastly, to you, the reader, thank you for trusting me with your time and your heart. I hope this journey blesses you with strength, understanding, and renewed faith.

THE TRAUMA DETOX

There comes a point in every hurting soul's journey when you wonder if true healing is possible. When the nights are long, your heart is weary, and you're desperate for a pathway out of the shadows. This is why the trauma detox was created. **The Trauma Detox** is a three-book sequence that speaks to that longing. It walks with you through the realities of trauma, helps in the process of daily rebuilding, and brings you to the exhilarating release of stepping into a life full of light and meaning.

In these books, you'll find more than just words on pages. You'll discover a map through a territory many hesitate to name—a map that doesn't promise instant fixes but steady progress anchored in faith and practical steps. We call it a "detox" because trauma, like toxins, can settle deeply into your mind, your body, and your spirit. Throughout these three books, we'll guide you as you uncover the residue of old wounds, release their stranglehold on your life, and watch your heart blossom into fresh possibilities.

- **Scarred** is where it all begins. It's like shining a flashlight into a darkened room, exposing the piled-up debris of hurt, betrayal, and fear. This first book recognizes the depth and weight of trauma without sugarcoating it. It invites you to confront what you may have once shoved aside—to name your aches, triggers, and silent grief. And even in the naming, you'll find the gentle beginnings of hope. The hope is that God sees every scar and whispers in your ear, *"Your pain is valid, but it doesn't have to be your identity."*

- **Mended** is the day-by-day progression—the second step in the journey where you learn routines, faith-based exercises, and fresh habits that help ease the burden you've carried. If *Scarred* asks you to name the wound, *Mended* shows you how to dress it, clean it, and let it heal properly. It's not a quick patch; it's a steady weave of prayer, community support, and practical strategies that loosen trauma's grip on your mind and body.

- **Bloom** represents the unfolding of a life that dares to move from just surviving to truly thriving. Here, the final stage of the detox becomes apparent as you discover new depths of joy, purpose, and outward impact. Rather than letting your scars define your boundaries, you learn to let them be symbols of strength—evidence that you've weathered storms and still have abundant life to live.

The healing process of the toxins of trauma in our bloodstream is a purging of what poisons our peace and a cleansing that can be both liberating and tenderly painful. Each book offers a different facet of this cleansing, ensuring you don't merely treat symptoms but address the core of your wound. Through scriptural insights, personal reflection, and an authentic, empathetic tone, we guide you gently but firmly toward wholeness.

Now, as you begin *Scarred*, you're stepping onto the first step of a ladder that leads out of the depths of trauma. This is where you bravely face the past so that it no longer dictates your future. Along the way, you'll be reminded that you are not alone: many have walked this path of naming their hurt, grieving their losses, and finding freedom on the other side. With each page, let your spirit open—trusting that the God who sees your scars also holds the key to your healing. Let the journey commence, for your life beyond trauma awaits.

INTRODUCTION

My friend, I don't know all that led you here, but I do know this: every scar on your soul and every wound in your heart is not the end of your story. While you might still be feeling the sting of yesterday's trauma, you must realize that it did not take you out. You are still here—reading, searching, daring to hope. That alone is a sign of life stirring in places you once thought lifeless.

I want you to imagine standing at the threshold of a new season. Yes, your past happened. Yes, the pain was real. But there is a stirring deep inside you, an undeniable sense that your scars don't have to define you, and they can become the first words of a powerful testimony.

In *Scarred*, we will walk together through honesty, heartache, and, ultimately, a gentle but firm path toward healing. This journey isn't about pretending life never hurt you. It's about letting God's love—steady and unchanging—touch each unseen wound, each hidden bruise, and lift you into renewed wholeness.

When you look at a scar, it often reminds you of how it got there, right? A fall you took, a choice you made, a betrayal you endured. But there's another side: that scar also says you survived. You overcame. You're still here. And what a miracle that is. Each chapter of this book is designed to bring that truth to the forefront of your mind and anchor it in your heart.

Maybe you're weary of advice that oversimplifies your pain: "Just get over it" or "Focus on the positive." You've tried, and it never seems enough. My friend, this is different. I won't offer quick fixes or pretend the past is quickly erased. Instead, I'll challenge you to face those wounds with the courage God has planted in you. You'll discover that broken places can birth resilience, and old tears can water new growth.

No matter how bleak your background or how lingering your pain, there is a path forward. Through personal stories, faith-based insights, and honest reflection, we'll explore why trauma clings so tightly—and how to loosen its grip. We'll learn to clarify those hidden hurts so they lose the power to haunt you and affect your life. We'll talk about the body and mind, how they hold on to trauma's residue, and how to gently release it.

This book is the starting point—a tender excavation of the places where pain took root. Here, you'll find tools that empower you to recognize what's been holding you back. You'll learn how your scars can become doorways to a richer experience of life, not roadblocks shutting you down. Together, we will invite the presence of God—who heals the brokenhearted and binds up every wound—into every page, every exercise, every silent prayer you whisper in the dark.

If your soul has felt cramped by shame, if your nights have been interrupted by flashbacks or silent dread, if your relationships have suffered because trust feels impossible—know that these pages are filled with unwavering hope. You are not alone. God sees you, cares for you, and has already poured strength into you that your trauma cannot steal.

So, let us begin this sacred process of acknowledging what hurts, naming what's been hidden, and witnessing a shift deep within. Picture the seed beneath a hardened patch of earth: it seems buried and forgotten, but with the right conditions, it will push up through the dirt into the light. Your soul's potential is far greater than any scar on your history.

Welcome to *Scarred*. Welcome to a safe place where we confront the unspoken, explore the unseen, and place each fragment of your story in the hands of the One who can weave beauty from brokenness. Whether you're trembling with uncertainty or burning with curiosity, I invite you to turn the page. Lean in. Trust that hope is more than a vague concept; it is the lifeline pulling you from the shadows.

Remember this: a scar is not the end of you. It's the evidence that you faced the darkness—and you're still standing. Let's walk through the healing journey, step by steady step until your heart holds more peace than pain, more faith than fear, and more life than any past wound could ever silence.

PROOF OF HEALING

Maya's Story

I didn't know how heavy my past was until it started spilling into every part of my life.

I'd learned to survive by staying silent. Every bruise and every sharp word caused me to cry myself to sleep almost every night. The next day, I would wake up trying my best to be jolly because I buried all the pain and anxiety deep. I used to smile through it. I Built walls so high that I forgot what was behind them. But the pain? It never forgot me.

When I first sat with Dr. Ivon Valerie, I didn't want to discuss my past. I was ashamed of it; I thought, "If I left it buried, it would not bother me." I wanted quick fixes for my panic attacks, trust issues, and constant self-doubt. I thought if I could "get over it," I'd be fine.

But Dr. Valerie didn't hand me a bandage. He gave me the truth.

I remember the day he said, "Your scars aren't a sign of defeat. They're proof that you survived what tried to break you." That was the first time

I didn't feel shame about my past. That day, I felt strength replaced years of shame.

He walked with me and helped me to get through the hard work. Work like naming my pain, facing the memories I buried, and understanding why my body reacted before my mind did. Saying it wasn't easy is not even close to how difficult this journey has been. What I have learned during this is trauma doesn't politely raise its hand and wait for permission to interrupt your life; it shouts through our panic, anger, fears, and insecurities. However, Dr. Valerie's guidance taught me how to quiet that storm.

I stopped seeing my scars as ugly reminders and started seeing them as battle wounds that prove I'm still standing. I've accepted that this journey wasn't about forgetting my past but reclaiming it. If you're carrying wounds, visible or invisible, I want you to know this: You are not broken beyond repair. There's strength in your scars waiting to be seen.

Maya (Name changed for privacy)

CHAPTER 1

UNDERSTANDING TRAUMA

You wake up some mornings with memories that feel like an unwanted guest—memories of events that robbed you of peace and cast shadows over your sense of safety. That weight you carry, the heaviness that grips your soul, is what we often call trauma. But what is trauma, truly? Too frequently, we use the word without understanding its depth. Trauma isn't a fleeting wound; it's an imprint on your soul, demanding understanding, faith, and healing.

Trauma is an experience so overwhelming that your body, mind, and spirit struggle to process it. It's not just the event but how your inner world absorbs and stores it. Picture your spirit as a woven complexity, each thread holding your emotional and spiritual well-being together.

Trauma tears at that fabric, sometimes unraveling it completely, leaving gaps that disrupt your sense of identity and security.

We often think of trauma as catastrophic events—a brutal assault, a life-threatening accident, or the horrors of war. But trauma also wears quieter faces. A child raised under a barrage of belittling words like "You'll never amount to anything." A teenager is bullied daily, dreading every school break. An adult enduring constant workplace harassment. These experiences may not make headlines, but their impact can weigh just as heavily on the soul. Trauma is not about the event's size but its effect on your sense of safety, worth, and belonging.

Two people can endure the same storm yet emerge with different stories. One processes the experience through prayer and supportive relationships, while the other remains haunted by nightmares and relentless fear. This isn't about strength or weakness but how our unique systems handle distress. Trauma is deeply personal. It's not measured by the severity of the event but by how it saturates your emotional core. If something left you feeling helpless, violated, or unsafe, and that feeling lingers, it's trauma.

Trauma disrupts your sense of normalcy. For the soldier haunted by war's explosions, the child witnessing domestic violence, or the assault survivor reliving the violation, the trauma reshapes their world. The same is true for someone repeatedly told they are worthless or constantly humiliated. These experiences leave scars not easily seen but deeply felt.

Even what we dismiss as "less dramatic" can be traumatic. A betrayal by a close friend. A public humiliation. These moments fracture trust, dignity, and self-worth, lodging themselves in your spirit. Don't minimize your story. Trauma isn't about whether others deem your pain valid; it's about how it shapes your heart and life.

Misconceptions about trauma are barriers to healing. Some believe that if you can't recall every detail, it wasn't "that bad." Others think to survive physically means you're fine emotionally. These myths silence those who need help, adding shame where there should be compassion. Trauma doesn't always come with clear memories. Some remember in vivid detail; others recall in fragments. Memory lapses don't erase the reality of trauma. Healing begins when we acknowledge the pain and seek support through counseling, faith-based groups, or trusted relationships.

Trauma can also challenge faith. You might ask, "Why did God allow this?" or "Have I been abandoned?" These questions can drive some away from the church, struggling to reconcile a good God with deep pain. Yet, faith doesn't ignore trauma; it meets it head-on. Scarred for humanity, the wounded Christ offers a picture of a God who understands personal pain. Even as you cry out in anger or confusion, you can encounter God's presence that comforts, restores, and strengthens.

My friend, scripture doesn't shy away from trauma. Think about Joseph, betrayed by his brothers and sold into slavery. Think of Naomi, who lost her husband and sons in a foreign land. Their grief was immense, their suffering real. Yet God's redemptive plan turned their heartbreak into testimonies that blessed generations. Joseph's journey from the pit to the palace wasn't instant but purposeful. Naomi's despair led to Ruth's lineage and the coming of Christ.

Your trauma, too, can have a greater purpose. This purpose doesn't erase the pain but reframes it. See, God can turn the darkest chapters of your life into altars of grace. The betrayal, loss, and fear can become part of a testimony that speaks of hope, healing, and redemption.

Healing from trauma requires courage. It's easier to hide behind denial than to confront the pain. But true healing begins with acknowledgment and action. Trauma doesn't define you. It's part of your story but not the end. With God's grace, the shattered pieces of your life can be reshaped into something beautiful. Your scars can testify to a healing God, a redeeming Savior, and a purpose bigger than your pain.

Reflection Questions

1. When you think of trauma, what's the first experience or feeling that rises in your heart? Why?

2. How has society's view of trauma shaped your understanding of your own pain?

3. Have you ever dismissed your trauma because "someone else had it worse"? How has that affected your healing?

4. In what ways has your trauma left invisible scars that others don't see?

5. What does it mean to you that God sees the wounds even you try to ignore?

6. How would your life change if you embraced your trauma not as your identity but as part of your journey?

CHAPTER 2

THE QUIET ACHE INSIDE

When you think of scars, you may visualize the shape of a particular wound or remember the moment you fell. You might touch that spot on your arm and flinch at the memory of how it happened. But for some of us—maybe for you—some scars aren't visible to anyone else. They've been imprinted into the quiet ache you feel during your morning commute or in the hush of night when your thoughts spin faster than you can hush them. These scars aren't embossed on your skin; they live in your memories, your emotions, and your body's reactions to everyday life. And even if the world doesn't see them, you carry them like a heavy bag you never asked to pack.

I want you to imagine something for a moment. Picture yourself standing in a dimly lit hallway lined with doors you've kept locked—stories and experiences that felt too painful or too confusing to face. Each door bears a label: Fear, Shame, Betrayal, Abandonment. Over time, you've grown accustomed to walking past these doors without a second thought because opening them felt like risking more pain. But in the stillness of certain nights, you sense a soft knock from the other side—a reminder that these wounds never vanished. They've gone underground, waiting for you to confront or continue carrying them in silence.

That's how trauma sneaks into our everyday rhythms. It settles into your shoulders, making them tense whenever a voice is raised. It creeps up in your dreams, jolting you awake in a puddle of sweat. It lingers in your chest, that tightness you feel whenever a memory resurfaces—an argument gone wrong, a betrayal that cut you deep, an experience that robbed you of your sense of safety. For so long, perhaps you believed that if you just pressed forward with a smile and put on your "I'm fine" mask, you could outrun the ghosts of your past.

But can I tell you something? Denial doesn't heal a wound; it stops you from cleaning it out. Pretending that ache isn't there only lets it fester. God didn't design you to limp through life burdened by unspoken sorrows. He created you with the capacity to heal, to transform, to stand tall even after life has tried to knock you down. And here, in this very moment, I believe you can take that first brave step: looking honestly at the scar—the invisible one that throbs in your mind and your memories—and allowing yourself to say, "I feel this. I'm tired of carrying it alone."

You see, trauma thrives in darkness. It tells you, "Don't let anyone see this shame." It whispers that your pain is too much for others to handle or that if they truly knew the depth of your hurt, they might walk away. But I want you to hear a different voice, one that gently insists, "You are not defined by what wounded you. Your scars are not proof of defeat but evidence that you survived." Survival is not the end of your story—there is more life for you beyond mere survival.

Sometimes, the body tries to tell you the truth even when your mind can't face it. Your jaw clenches at a memory, or your heart pounds when a specific name is mentioned. You wonder why you're so tense, why certain moments trigger anxiety or tears out of nowhere. My dear friend, that's your body shouting, "Something happened here." Our physical frame carries trauma like a silent partner waiting for your acknowledgment. When you finally look it in the face and say, "I see you, I hear you," you open the door for peace to walk in. When your mind and body align, healing becomes more than just a wish—it becomes a tangible possibility.

Let me remind you that God is not distant from your aching places. He doesn't watch your tears from afar, unmoved. God leans in close, His heart aching with yours. The Psalmist says that He is near to the brokenhearted—and oh, how comforting to realize that He's not waiting for you to "get it together," He's waiting for you to let Him in. That quiet ache is an invitation to let God's love saturate every hidden wound, to allow the comforting presence of the Holy Spirit to bring warmth where you've felt cold and alone.

Stepping into this journey means you'll encounter resistance—old shame might rise, or fear might try to silence your progress. But each time you name that fear, you weaken its hold. Each time you offer up a whispered prayer—"Lord, this still hurts, but I trust You,"—you cater to the healing of your soul. This is not about sweeping your past under the rug; it's about taking your rightful place as someone destined to live, breathe, and thrive, not just endure.

It's brave to look at what caused that scar in your heart. But it's even more heroic to declare that it will not define you. From this day forward, I challenge you to notice when your body tenses, your heart begins to race, or when an old memory tries to rule your present. Gently remind yourself, "I am safe now. My scars no longer control me." That's the whisper of truth that paves the road to restoration.

So, in these moments, let honesty guide you as you read and reflect. Write down what you feel, even if it's messy or tangled. Speak aloud the hurts you've buried; let tears flow if they come. And hold on to this promise: your scars can transform into stories of hope. They can become indicators that you endured, yet by grace, you are still standing.

God sees you. He loves you unconditionally. And He's here, ready to walk with you through every memory, every hidden ache, until your nights grow calmer and your days shine with renewed joy. The quiet ache inside you doesn't have the final word—because healing, courage, and faith are more potent than any trauma that tried to break you.

Welcome to the journey. Let's step forward together, trusting that each scar is a stepping stone, each tear is a release, and each moment of truth opens the door for wholeness to flood in. This chapter is just the start of uncovering that quiet ache, laying it before the One who restores, and giving you permission to breathe again—deep and free. Let's walk into the light, my friend, for healing, awaits on the other side of your yes.

Reflection Questions

1. What parts of your story have you locked away in silence because the ache felt too deep to speak?

2. When was the last time you sat quietly with your emotions—without running, numbing, or distracting yourself?

3. What role has shame played in keeping your pain hidden?

4. Who do you feel safe enough to share your "quiet aches" with, and if no one, what's stopping you?

5. How does God meet you in those silent spaces where words feel too heavy?

CHAPTER 3

THE BODY REMEMBERS

Picture a young child startled awake by the boom of thunder. Even long after the storm passes, that child might flinch at the faintest rumble in the distance. Trauma is much the same way. You might stand in a serene place, no danger in sight, yet your body still trembles with echoes of what happened long ago. It's as if every muscle and heartbeat carries the imprint of past wounds. Whether we realize it or not, our bodies constantly try to tell us a story of where we've been and what we've survived.

Sometimes, you'll catch yourself tensing your shoulders or grinding your teeth when anxiety creeps in. Or maybe you notice your jaw clenches without you knowing why. It might happen when you're in a crowd or facing a simple decision that feels bigger than it should. Suddenly, you recognize your back hurts, your head pounds, your muscles ache. That tension isn't random. It's your body holding onto the memory of pain, betrayal, or fear—like a protective stance bracing for an impact that may never come again.

One dear friend shared how she walked around for years with her shoulders practically pinned to her ears. "I thought it was normal," she told me, "until I felt the relief of letting go." She would walk into a grocery store, hear a loud noise from an overhead speaker, and her entire torso would stiffen. Why? Because her body hadn't forgotten the environment where she had once felt threatened and powerless. It's extraordinary how these silent memories remain, waiting for the slightest resemblance to a past threat to resurface.

And it doesn't stop with tense shoulders. Maybe your heart starts racing when you're alone in the house, or your palms get clammy at the sound of someone raising their voice. Trauma sets off an alarm system that works a little too well. What was meant to keep you safe can now keep you trapped, believing every raised voice or quiet street at dusk is a repeat of what hurt you. You lie awake at night, exhausted but unable to rest, replaying scenes that feed your worry. Or you toss and turn, your stomach churning like bracing for an unseen blow.

See, the body doesn't forget easily. When we've walked through trauma—be it sudden or stretched over the years—our flesh and bones learn to anticipate danger. Sometimes, we shame ourselves for these physical reactions, thinking, "I shouldn't be so sensitive" or, "I'm weak for feeling this way." But you must realize this: these reactions are not weakness but signals. Your body is crying out, saying, "I remember something hurtful happened, and I don't want it to happen again."

What a beautiful and complicated creation we are. The same body that feels the Holy Spirit's warmth can also carry locked-up pain in its cells. But I want you to know that God, in His mercy, hasn't abandoned you to these tensions and triggers. He stands ready to guide you into understanding so that each ache, each skipped heartbeat, can be gently reworked into a testimony of healing. Instead of seeing these body memories as proof that you're hopelessly broken, you can see them as messengers that something in you still needs comfort and care.

Sometimes, acknowledging the body's story is the key to unlocking deeper levels of freedom. If you've been dealing with tightness in your chest, knots in your stomach, restless sleep—maybe it's time to pause and ask: "Body, what are you trying to tell me?" Because the remedy isn't just to push through or pretend you're okay; it's to slow down and let the Spirit of God breathe peace into every corner of your being. In a tense moment, it's choosing to whisper: "I'm safe now. I'm not in danger. The Lord is with me. My body can let go."

Letting go might seem too tall a task, especially if you've carried this tension for years. But letting go doesn't mean you deny that something terrible happened. It means you invite a greater truth—God's abiding presence and unwavering love—into the places your body has held onto pain. It may mean practicing simple, grace-filled acts: pausing to take slow, steady breaths, gently rolling your shoulders, placing a hand on your chest, and speaking kindness over yourself. These small choices echo a deeper spiritual truth: you can rest, feel safe, and release the burdens you were never meant to carry for so long.

In the hush of an anxious night, you might find yourself quietly reciting a verse that steadies your heart. Or, in the bustle of a busy workday, you could close your eyes for thirty seconds and recall that God is your protector. Over time, these deliberate acts of awareness remind your body that it doesn't have to stay in survival mode. You might begin noticing a softening in your demeanor or a moment when someone's loud laugh no longer sends your heart racing.

I remember a gentleman who, for years, couldn't sit in the back seat of a car. It reminded him of a traumatic event from his teens. Each time he tried, he'd sweat, his stomach would knot, and he'd feel the suffocating press of panic. He found he could gradually reclaim his freedom through prayer, gentle counseling, and exercises acknowledging his body's response. The process was neither quick nor easy, but it was a profound demonstration of how our bodies respond to old wounds—and how they can eventually learn a new way of being.

That is the journey I invite you to. It is not one of denying your body's alarms but of learning to comfort them and teach them the truth: You are safe, and healing is possible. God gave us these remarkable temples we call our bodies. Yes, sometimes they remember pain too well. But I believe they can also become instruments of worship and testimonies of grace. When your heart stops pounding, and your muscles ease from their rigid stance, you see evidence of the Holy Spirit ministering to the wounds beneath the surface.

So, when your shoulders rise, and your breath shortens, pause. Ask yourself: "What is this about? Lord, show me where I need reassurance." That simple question can usher in calm where there is panic. This is not mere positive thinking but the powerful act of acknowledging your body's feelings and inviting God's presence into that sensation. Over time, you'll learn that not every jolt or tightened muscle is a red flag; sometimes, it's just a memory seeking to be rewritten by God's gentle hand.

And let me reassure you: this isn't a one-and-done formula. The body's memory can be stubborn, especially when trauma runs deep. But grace abounds. Each day brings new opportunities to listen, pray, release tension, and declare that you are fearfully and wonderfully made and that your body can receive peace rather than stay locked in old patterns of distress.

As you move forward in these pages, carry this thought: your body is your ally, not your enemy. It's merely responding to the experiences you've endured. You affirm a new reality by learning to soothe and speak kindly to those tense muscles, that racing heart, or those sleepless nights. You declare, "I am not who I was when that trauma happened. I've grown. God has sustained me. I will not stay stuck in fear."

Let today mark a milestone where you begin to hear what your body is telling you, and you graciously respond with compassion and faith. Step by step, breath by breath, muscle by muscle, you are moving toward wholeness. And with every gentle shift, every prayer whispered in tension, you testify that trauma's memory is no match for the healing that awaits you in God's profound love.

Reflection Questions

1. Have you ever noticed how your body reacts before your mind catches up—tight shoulders, rapid heartbeat, a sinking feeling? What's your body trying to tell you?

2. In what ways has your body held onto trauma long after your mind tried to forget?

3. Reflect on a moment when your body responded in fear, anger, or anxiety—what was the deeper root of that reaction?

4. How often do you listen to your body's signals, and how often do you ignore them?

5. How can you begin treating your body as a partner in healing rather than a battlefield of pain?

CHAPTER 4

TRIGGERS EVERYWHERE

H ave you ever been caught off guard by a simple sound, a fragrance, or a passing image that instantly transports you back to a painful place? One moment, you're living your everyday life—pushing a cart through the grocery store, maybe humming a favorite tune—and the next, your body seizes up, your heart flutters, and your mind lands in the middle of an old battle you thought was long forgotten. That swift jag isn't your imagination; it's a trigger.

Triggers are those subtle reminders—like the smell of a particular cologne, a sudden burst of laughter that sounds just like someone who once hurt you, or the ominous hush of a house late at night. They're the cues that unlock past traumas and make the present moment feel as overwhelming as the original wound. We often ask, "Why am I reacting this way? I'm safe now, so what's wrong with me?" But let me tell you: nothing's wrong with you. This is how our hearts and bodies hold onto what's unresolved, alerting us to something we may not even realize we're carrying.

I recall a story of a friend who would catch the faintest whiff of smoke and immediately tense up, scanning the room for exits, breath quickening as though he stood in a burning building. In reality, he was completely safe—a fire crackling in someone's backyard several houses down. But because he once survived a house fire, that faint smell of smoke transported him to a moment of terror. Trauma doesn't politely knock on the door of our minds; it barges in any time it recognizes a reminder of the past.

Your triggers may appear during a harmless TV show when a scene suddenly matches something buried deep in your memory. Or perhaps it's a specific date on the calendar—the anniversary of an event so hurtful, you can almost feel your skin crawl just thinking about it. You might even find yourself reacting to a color, a texture, or a song lyric. And you wonder, "Why is this so powerful?" Because trauma records not just events but details, filing them away in the corners of your soul.

It can feel terribly unfair that your mind and body react this way, especially when you only want to move on. Yet triggers are not signs of weakness. In fact, they're your inner system trying to protect you, waving a red flag that something in this moment feels uncomfortably similar to what once harmed you. The challenge is distinguishing between an actual threat and a perceived one so you don't remain trapped in the panic of yesteryears.

But, friend, triggers don't have to dominate your life. Becoming aware of them is the first step toward freedom. You can begin to prepare your heart if you can name what sets off that wave of dread—whether it's a voice tone, a location, or a certain topic in conversation. Instead of getting blindsided, you can see the storm clouds forming and take shelter before the flash flood. And each time you do, you reinforce the truth that you are no longer living in that old trauma. The danger has passed, and though the memories remain, they do not rule over you.

I remember my friend Sharon felt a wave of panic every time she heard a door slam. She'd freeze in place, heart racing, ready to defend herself from an argument that wasn't even happening. When my friend finally realized door slams triggered a memory of her parents' angry shouts, she began carrying little affirmations in her phone—verses of comfort, short prayers, and calming statements. Each time that door-slam panic started, Sharon would take slow breaths and read those affirmations, reminding herself she was safe now. Over time, the intensity of those triggers softened. She dislikes loud door slams, but they no longer hijacked her day.

God is not surprised by our triggers. He understands the complexities of our minds and the tears behind every reaction. The Bible reminds us that He is close to the brokenhearted, intimately familiar with the delicateness of our grief. When triggers strike, it can be tempting to feel shame, like, "Why am I not over this yet?" But healing, my friend, is a journey—a layered process. With each trigger you face and respond to more healthily, you affirm a new truth: that your past does not have the final say.

One of the best ways to disarm triggers is to bring them into the light. Sometimes, telling a trustworthy friend or counselor, "I realize I get panicked when I hear people arguing," can loosen the grip that secret held on you. Confession is powerful: the moment you voice it, you shrink its power. And if you can go further—understanding that the trigger is tied to a specific moment or pattern in your history—you give yourself the space to heal that wound rather than hiding it.

It's also important to remember that managing triggers doesn't mean ignoring them. Suppose a certain movie scene makes you tremble or a certain restaurant floods you with bad memories. In that case, your knee-jerk reaction might be to avoid them altogether. There's no shame in wisely avoiding situations that re-traumatize you, especially in the early stages of healing. But eventually, many find that gently re-introducing some of those elements—this time with prayer, support, and new coping tools—can reshape the emotional landscape so the trigger loses its power.

You might develop practical strategies, like carrying a small comforting item in your pocket—a smooth stone, a note card with a Scripture, or a photograph that reminds you of safety. So when that old fear stirs, you can reach into your pocket, hold that object, and remind yourself, "I'm secure, I'm loved, I'm in the present moment." That simple action can ground you, keeping you tethered to now instead of drifting into the seas of the past. It's a tangible way to confront the old panic with the truth of your current reality.

Sometimes, triggers demand more work—counseling sessions or therapy with someone skilled at unraveling trauma's knots. There is no shame in seeking that help. If you fell and broke a bone, you'd see a doctor. Likewise, you deserve supportive care if your soul and spirit are bruised. A coach or counselor can help you systematically face and process the events feeding your triggers so you eventually walk freely without the dread of old memories roaring back.

And let's not forget the immense comfort found in spiritual support. Prayer groups, friends of faith, pastors—people who'll stand with you when the shadows of yesterday reach out to darken your today. Their prayers can fortify you, helping you stand firm when triggers attempt to yank you off balance. With each prayed word, you declare that your future belongs to hope, not to the haunting echoes of what broke you.

If you're reading this and feeling overwhelmed because triggers seem everywhere—like landmines you can't avoid—take heart. Even if you can't control every trigger, you can learn to influence how you respond. You can choose, moment by moment, to breathe in God's peace rather than letting panic govern you. Yes, it's a learning curve, but you are more resilient than you realize.

At first, triggers might feel like unstoppable waves crashing against your shore. But with time and intentional healing, the tide begins to recede. The day will come when that song, that smell, that date on the calendar no longer paralyzes you. Maybe you'll still feel a faint twinge, a soft pang of memory—but you'll be able to exhale, ground yourself in prayer, and keep going. We're working toward a life where your triggers are recognized but do not reign, where your painful past never drowns the beauty of your present.

So keep your heart encouraged, beloved. Name your triggers without shame. Seek God's counsel in every reaction, leaning on supportive relationships and practical tools. Watch how the presence of the Holy Spirit comforts those bruised areas, slowly guiding you to see that triggers, while potent, are not permanent chains. You are stepping into a season of reclaiming territory once owned by fear. And as you walk through these triggers, you strengthen the truth that you are greater than what happened to you, braver than the ghosts of your past, and deeply, profoundly loved by the One who calls you forward.

Reflection Questions

1. What people, places, or situations unexpectedly trigger memories of your trauma?

2. How have your triggers made you feel powerless—and how can you reclaim that power?

3. When you're triggered, do you respond with compassion toward yourself, or do you spiral into shame?

4. Have you ever let a trigger stop you from moving forward? How can you challenge that pattern?

5. What's one healthy coping strategy you can use the next time you're caught off guard by a trigger?

CHAPTER 5

THE WEIGHT OF SILENCE

J ean, a gentleman I met in Guadeloupe, explained that he usually felt like he was carrying a secret so heavy that it made his entire body ache. He went on to explain that day after day, he walked around with this invisible burden, silently hoping no one noticed the strain on his shoulders or the tiredness in his eyes. This conversation came about because I saw the tiredness in his eyes and asked him about it while we were having lunch. Maybe you can identify with Jean. Perhaps you go through life putting on your best face—nodding politely, cracking a half-smile, uttering "I'm okay"—all the while, a thousand unspoken truths press against your chest. That dear reader, is the weight of silence: the unvoiced pain that steals your breath and keeps you feeling alone, even in a crowd.

Silence has a way of growing heavier with time. What starts as a small, hidden wound can become a massive ache if left unspoken. A scripture in Proverbs says anxiety in a person's heart weighs them down, but a kind word cheers them up. Imagine how silence magnifies that anxiety: when you hide your story, your trauma, and your fears, you're essentially feeding them in the dark. Where honesty and light could soothe your mind, secrecy keeps you bound.

I heard of a woman who held her trauma like a prisoner in a dark cell. She was convinced she would lose her fragile control over her life if she spoke of it and let the words pass her lips. She kept her voice locked away for years. Her face would tighten whenever anyone tried to get close to her pain. But the quiet was choking her, slowly robbing her of authentic joy. A simple question about her past made her pulse race; she scrambled for excuses to avoid conversations that grazed even the edges of her sorrow. The burden of not speaking had become heavier than the wound itself.

Perhaps you've felt that way, too—if you dared to speak about what really happened, people would think less of you. Or worse, they'd blame, judge, or dismiss your heartache as "dramatic." Yet there's an old saying: we are only as sick as our secrets. When we refuse to name our pain, we give it permission to grow like mold in a dark room. But the moment we open a window and let some fresh air in, that mold can't flourish. In the same manner, the moment you begin to voice your story—even if only to a single trusted friend—the suffocating power of that wound starts losing its grip.

It's important to note that sharing does not mean broadcasting your business to every stranger on the street. It's about finding someone—a compassionate friend, a counselor, a spiritual leader—who can hold your truth without dismissing it or exploiting it. Because there's something liberating about hearing your voice say, "This happened to me. It hurt, and I'm tired of pretending it didn't." In that moment, you take the first step toward freedom. The fear that once caged, you start showing its cracks because you realize you're no longer in it alone.

Think about it: in Genesis, when Adam and Eve first sinned, they hid themselves, covering up with fig leaves. Shame and silence go hand in hand. Our pain and our guilt tempt us to hide—be it behind a forced grin, nonstop busyness, or isolation. But God, in His tenderness, asks, "Where are you?" Not because He doesn't know, but because speaking up—revealing yourself—is the path to reconnecting with God, the One who can help you heal. So when you feel that urge to remain silent, consider that maybe God is gently asking, "Where are you, child? Let me meet you in your brokenness."

Now, there's a risk in speaking, isn't there? If you confide in the wrong person, the pain might compound. That's why discernment matters. But, friend, don't let the fear of being misunderstood keep you locked in silence forever. Sometimes, you must keep searching for that safe person or group—a faith-based support circle, a wise counselor, a trusted mentor—until you find the right space where your story can land softly. It may take some trial and error, but it's worth the effort for the relief and clarity that follows genuine confession and sharing.

You might wonder, "But what if I speak my story, and it hurts just as much to say it out loud?" The truth is, speaking your pain can indeed be uncomfortable in the moment. Tears might come, or trembling might grip you. But that discomfort is often the necessary labor pain leading you into a new birth. On the other side of that release, many discover a profound lightness. It's like you finally exhale after holding your breath for too long. You realize, "Yes, it happened, but it doesn't own me. Yes, I was wounded, but I'm still standing."

And let's talk about shame. Shame thrives in silence. It feeds on the belief that if people "really knew," they'd reject you or deem you unworthy of love. But here's the thing about shame: it cannot survive the light of honest empathy. When someone looks you in the eye and says, "I hear you. I'm so sorry you went through that," shame starts backing away, hissing like a cornered snake. This is why spiritual community, genuine friendship, and prayerful support can be so transformative. They offer a mirror reflecting God's compassion instead of judgment, showing you that your worth has never been questioned.

Sometimes, you might not be ready to speak to someone else. That's understandable. You can start by writing a journal entry, a letter you may or may not send. Pour out the feelings you've guarded all these years. Name the hurt, the anger, the sorrow, the confusion. Write until your hand cramps if you need to. Then, bring that paper into a prayerful moment: "Lord, this is my truth. I'm not hiding anymore. Guide me to the next step." Even that act of self-disclosure breaks the chains of secrecy in your own soul.

The weight of silence can feel like a thousand pounds pressing down on your spirit, but each word spoken and each truth revealed lifts it ounce by ounce. You might not see the complete difference immediately. But day by day, you'll notice you stand straighter and breathe more freely. And in time, you may look back and marvel at how silence once caged you and how your choice to speak peeled back the bars, letting hope slip in.

You were not fashioned for concealment; you were created for connection. Your story, whether it's messy or neat, whether it's still raw or partially healed, carries value beyond measure. Silence tries to bury that story in a grave of shame and fear. But God is in the business of resurrection—He calls forth life from dead places. That includes the buried truths in your heart. As you allow them to surface and exchange secrecy for honest vulnerability, you position yourself for a resurrection of your soul.

Yes, vulnerability is risky. But staying silent robs you of the healing, the empathy, and the closeness you crave. It keeps you tied to the myth that you must handle everything independently. Take a leap of faith, even a small one, and let a trusted voice hear your story. It may be just a piece of it, just a start. But it's enough to begin turning that boulder of silence into a pathway to restoration.

So ask yourself tonight, or whenever your mind is quiet: "What have I been carrying that I need to name out loud?" Maybe it's an incident of abuse, a moment of abandonment, or even guilt over something you regret. Let it no longer hold you hostage in the recesses of your heart.

Open the door a bit, let the light of truth flood in, and watch how the shadows that once loomed so large begin to shrink under the weight of genuine honesty and God's gentle grace.

Silence may have weighed on you for years, but a single choice to speak can change the entire landscape of your inner world. You don't have to broadcast your past to everyone—just to someone who can handle it with compassion and discretion. That first conversation might feel like standing at the edge of a cliff. But once you take the step, you'll find that you're not falling into darkness; you're leaping into a liberating new chapter of your life.

May the weight of silence no longer press upon your soul. May the truth you speak lead you into the arms of God, whose love is big enough to hold every hurt, every tear, and every sigh of relief that comes from finally laying down this burden. Because once you shed that weight, you stand ready to receive the healing you deserve, the empathy you've longed for, and the joy waiting on the other side of your honest voice.

Reflection Questions

1. Think of a time when your silence spoke louder than words. What was the cost of that silence?

2. How has keeping your pain hidden affected your relationships with others—and with God?

3. What fears rise up when you think about sharing your story out loud?

4. Are you holding onto secrets that are keeping you in emotional or spiritual bondage?

5. How does knowing that your voice has the power to bring healing challenge the way you live your truth?

CHAPTER 6

YOU ARE NOT ALONE

H ave you ever walked through a crowded place—bustling streets, a busy office, even a church foyer—yet felt profoundly alone? Like everyone else has somewhere to belong, someone to lean on, while you carry your burdens without a hand to hold? That sense of isolation can feel heavier than the trauma itself. It whispers, *"Nobody understands... you're all alone in this."* But let me tell you something, beloved: that is a lie. You are not alone, even when loneliness would have you believe otherwise.

You might look around and think other people's lives are calm, collected, and free of baggage. From the outside, their smiles or social media posts seem effortless. But behind so many of those smiles, there are hidden scars—unspoken stories of broken trust, childhood anguish, abusive re-lationships, or life-shattering disappointments. Countless souls walk this earth carrying weights that look different from yours but weigh just as much. The truth is, you are not the only one who's been wounded. You are among the many fighting, surviving, and—by God's grace—learning to thrive despite the pain.

Statistics may tell us that a staggering number of adults experience trauma in one form or another. But beyond the numbers, we see living, breathing people. Their stories are diverse—someone might have endured the chaos of an unstable home, another wrestle with flashbacks from a horrific accident, and yet another battle the fallout of a loved one's betrayal. Across all these differences, one thread ties them together: the need to feel heard, understood, and supported.

When you realize how many people carry hidden wounds, something remarkable happens: shame loses its edge. The enemy of our souls would like you to believe your pain is unique in its darkness or that your struggles brand you as weak or broken beyond repair. But in Scripture, God places us in community for a reason. Elijah once felt alone, convinced he was the only prophet left who hadn't bowed to idols—but God reminded him there were seven thousand others in Israel who stood faithful. *You are not alone either.* God has people—yes, a community—set aside for you, too.

It could be a support group at a local church, a circle of friends who gather for prayer, or an online community where survivors share their journeys. Sometimes, you'll encounter a mentor or counselor who's walked a similar road and found healing on the other side. Their empathy becomes a balm you've longed for, and you hear the echo of your own experiences in their voice. Suddenly, you realize you're in a room where you no longer have to pretend. There, your story is met with nods of understanding, maybe even tears that mirror your own.

Oh, what a difference that can make! Imagine carrying a heavy weight on your shoulders, stumbling under the load, and feeling the ache in your back. Then, someone lifts part of that burden, easing the strain. That's what the right community does for you. They pray for you when your words fail, check in when the nights get long, and remind you of hope when darkness tries to pull you back into depression. Their presence testifies that God never intended you to fight these battles alone.

Maybe you've convinced yourself, "No one can handle my truth," or "I'm not sure I can trust anyone." If that's you, I urge you to take a small step. Sometimes, it's as simple as sharing your story with a trusted friend or a counselor. You don't have to unload everything at once—just let someone see behind your carefully curated image. The first time might feel frightening, but more often than not, that caring friend or mentor will gently receive your words, respond with grace, and prove that your story is worth hearing.

You might ask, "But what if I've tried to open up before, and people didn't understand, or they used my vulnerability against me?" Sadly, betrayal can happen, even in spiritual settings. We are humans and we can fail. Yet don't let past disappointments condemn you to a life of solitary struggles. Keep praying for discernment and seeking a safe space. Sometimes, you must knock on a few doors before you find the one that opens to the right environment for your healing. Believe me, there is somebody—maybe it's a pastor who's walked through trauma themselves or a friend who has deeper empathy than you ever realized—who can share your load.

In Galatians, we read, "Bear one another's burdens, and so fulfill the law of Christ." That's not just a sentimental phrase; it's an instruction. We were meant to show up for each other—because when you feel known and supported, those triggers we talked about become less crippling, and that silent ache loses its sting. When you hear another soul say, "I've been there too," a powerful sense of relief unfolds. Your heart whispers, *I'm not crazy, I'm not overreacting—someone else gets it.* And that moment is worth all the courage it takes to escape isolation.

Sometimes, you'll find genuine community in unlikely places. I've seen healing happen in small Bible studies, recovery groups, or even among co-workers sharing a meal on their lunch breaks. I've seen it unfold in late-night phone calls between two friends who decided to be honest about their depression or anxiety. I've witnessed families mend once they acknowledge the unspoken wounds passed from generation to generation. This sense of shared experience can dismantle the lie that your pain is too ugly or complicated for others to handle.

If you've been burned by churches or religious folks who didn't listen, please don't give up on the possibility of a faith-based community that will love you as Christ loves you. Every congregation has flaws, but there are places where wounded people are met with compassion. Seek out pastors or leaders who preach grace and model empathy. Seek out believers who talk openly about their battles and victories, who won't shame you for your scars but welcome you into the fellowship of shared healing.

Above all, remember that even when we fail, God never does. His constant promise is: *"I will never leave or forsake you."* You have a Father who sees every tear, reads every trembling thought, and stands ready to guide you toward the necessary connections. Sometimes, the Holy Spirit will lead you to the right person and group at the right time. You might see a flyer for a support meeting that catches your eye, or a friend might mention a therapist who understands trauma. Pay attention to those small nudges—they could be the divine breadcrumbs guiding you to the place where your heart can finally breathe.

Don't let shame, doubt, or the lie that "nobody cares" keep you from discovering the power of shared experiences. Your healing journey is not meant to be a lonely one. Isolation makes trauma feel bigger, but community puts it into perspective. It's humbling yet profoundly comforting to realize you're part of a vast network of people who've survived life's brutal twists and turns and found hope beyond it all.

Yes, you are not alone. It's a phrase we often hear, but I pray it settles in your spirit as a living truth. You are not the only one carrying hidden scars; you are not the only one who sometimes feels overwhelmed by the past. Across this world, in different languages and cultures, people are taking the same brave steps to confront their trauma. They also find that freedom emerges when hearts unite in vulnerability and faith.

As you lean into this leg of your journey, let the knowledge of shared struggle be a balm to your soul. Seek out others who can walk alongside you—don't try to trek every rocky path by yourself. Learn from their stories, and dare to share pieces of yours. The body of Christ is beautifully diverse and richly equipped with comforting arms, wise voices, and listening ears. Step into the circle of fellowship where your burdens are halved and your joys are multiplied.

You are not alone, my friend. You never have been. And by embracing divine and human connection, you'll discover a sense of belonging that speaks louder than any old trauma voice telling you otherwise. Let that truth wash over you. Let it loosen the knot in your chest. Let it remind you that there's a seat at the table of grace with your name on it, surrounded by others who understand and by a God who loves you beyond measure.

Reflection Questions

1. In what moments of your life did you feel the most isolated? How did that isolation impact your healing?

2. How has the belief that "no one understands me" shaped your relationships?

3. Who has been a safe presence in your life during difficult seasons? What made them feel safe?

4. How has God shown up in moments when you felt completely alone—even if you didn't notice it at the time?

5. What's holding you back from fully embracing community as part of your healing journey?

CHAPTER 7

FAITH AS A STEADY LIGHT

P icture yourself standing in a darkened room, groping for a way out. The shadows feel endless, and every step forward feels unsteady and uncertain. Then, with the strike of a match, a gentle flame flickers to life. It doesn't chase away all the darkness at once but illuminates enough for you to see the next step. That slight glow becomes your guide, your steady companion through what feels like a maze of fear.

That's what faith is like amid trauma. It doesn't erase every painful memory or magically remove every scar; instead, it provides a light that leads you through the unknown. If trauma whispers, "You'll never see beyond this pain," faith softly answers, "I'm with you, even here."

We often imagine faith as reserved for grand celebrations or bold mira-cles. But it's most profound when we're standing on shaky ground. Some nights, you lie awake, mind flooded with worries, regrets, or flashbacks. In the hush of your darkest hours, it's then that even a seed of faith can become a lifeline. You might not yet see the grand horizon of healing, but faith ensures you can see enough to keep moving forward, one courageous step at a time.

Remember, a verse in Scripture says we walk by faith, not sight. When trauma clouds your vision, robbing your ability to see hope, it's faith that guides you through. Faith in a God who doesn't abandon you in the valley; your story is bigger than the chapter you're living in now; faith that your broken places aren't irreparable in the hands of the One who created you. It's this steady light that helps you breathe again when panic threatens. It reminds you you're safe in God's arms even when old nightmares resurface.

You might say, "But my faith feels so small. I doubt. I question. I'm angry at times." Hear me: God is not fragile. He can handle your doubts and your questions. In fact, those honest cries can bring you closer to Him because genuine faith isn't about having all the answers. It's about holding onto the truth that even in your confusion, there's a Presence guiding you, comforting you, and breathing strength into your weary bones.

Faith isn't wishful thinking. It's not a denial of the trauma you've expe-rienced. Instead, it's an anchor that keeps you from drifting away when storms rage. Think of a boat battered by waves. It would be swept off course without an anchor, lost to the relentless sea. Yet, with an anchor, it stays tethered to a solid point. That's what your faith does—it tethers your heart to God's promises, even when your emotions are on a violent roller coaster. It says, "I may be swaying, but I will not be carried away."

Consider the moments when triggers flare up—the pounding heart, the tremors in your hands, the voice of old fears echoing in your mind. In those moments, faith offers a different voice. It can be as simple as a prayer: "Lord, I feel fear rising, but I trust You are with me." Or a Scripture verse: "You are my refuge and my fortress; in You I trust." That might not instantly remove every trace of anxiety. But it shifts your focus from the looming threat to the Lord, who is bigger than anything that happened to you.

There is power in inviting God into the rawest parts of your story. Trauma tries to convince you that those wounds are too ugly, too shameful. Yet faith says, "God, here's my brokenness. Please pour Your grace into it." Over time, you discover that grace seeps into the cracks of your soul, healing wounds you thought would never stop bleeding. It doesn't always happen overnight, but little by little, as you keep bringing your hurts into God's presence, He reworks them into testimonies of His redemption.

Do you remember the woman in the Gospels who had been bleeding for twelve years? She pushed through the crowd to touch the hem of Jesus' garment, believing that even that tiny contact would bring healing. Trauma can feel like a twelve-year bleeding of the heart. But if you reach out—through prayer, worship, and quiet moments of surrender—you're essentially saying, "If I can just touch His presence, I can find hope again." The beauty is that God notices even that slight, trembling reach. He meets you in your desperation and responds with mercy.

Faith also thrives in community. Sometimes, we borrow each other's faith. Maybe you've been too weary to pray for yourself or ashamed to see any goodness ahead. That's where a faithful friend, pastor, or small group can step in. Their prayers can be the strong arms holding up yours when you're too exhausted to lift them to heaven. Their words can be reminders of God's promises when your own mind feels foggy with despair. Lean on them; let them help stoke that flicker of faith in you until it grows into a flame.

And even if your faith is just a spark right now, don't underestimate its potential. A match can light a candle that disperses shadows; a single candle can brighten a whole room. Likewise, a seed of faith can grow into a bold confidence that your trauma doesn't define your future. The day may come when you say, "Yes, I walked through the valley of darkness, but I found a Light that never flickered out."

You can nurture this faith by weaving it into your daily routines. Maybe you start mornings with a quick Scripture verse or a simple prayer—thanking God for breath in your lungs, inviting Him into your healing process. Perhaps you listen to uplifting worship music on your commute or journal your prayers before bed. Over time, these small acts create an environment where faith flourishes, keeping you attuned to divine guidance rather than stuck in the replay of old wounds.

Don't worry if you still have doubts or if the darkness seems to hide that light some days. Faith isn't about never doubting; it's about continuing to move forward, trusting that God will guide your feet even if your hands are trembling. It's about that quiet resolve that says, "I'm not giving up. I believe there's more for me than this pain." And in God's hands, that humble declaration can spark miracles of transformation in the most battered parts of your soul.

So when you feel trapped again when the ache of trauma resurfaces, whisper this truth to yourself: *Faith is my steady light.* Let it speak to your fear; let it comfort your heart. Let it draw you closer to the God who knows your tears and cares about each one. Over time, you'll find that faith helps you navigate trauma and invites you to a new level of closeness with the Lord—where you experience His grace in places you never thought could be redeemed.

Yes, trauma tried to cast a shadow over your life, but faith shines brighter. The steady light guides you toward a future filled with wholeness, joy, and purpose—even if you can't see all the details yet. All you need is enough light for the next step. And that, dear friend, is what faith provides. Lean into it, nurture it, and watch how it grows, illuminating your path day by day and never ceasing to remind you that healing is not just possible—it's already in motion.

Reflection Questions

1. When has your faith been the most fragile in your healing journey, and what helped it hold on?

2. How do you wrestle with the tension between trusting God's timing and wanting immediate healing?

3. What does "walking by faith, not by sight" look like in the middle of trauma recovery?

4. When you feel like you're drowning in pain, what anchors your faith?

5. Reflect on a moment when God showed up for you in a way you didn't expect. How did it shift your understanding of His love?

CHAPTER 8

Step By Step Toward Healing

There's a story told of a traveler hiking up a rugged mountain path. Each step feels like a small triumph—rocks shift beneath the boots, muscles ache, and sweat beads on the brow. But with each foot planted, the traveler gains another inch of ground, another moment closer to the summit. Healing from trauma is much like that climb. It doesn't happen in a single leap but through a series of faithful steps, each building upon the last.

You may look at your life now and wonder, *"How far have I come?"* Perhaps the daily grind of anxiety, the sudden jolts of triggers, or the lingering heaviness of past wounds has you feeling like progress is slow or nonexistent. But here's the truth: every time you face a trigger and respond with a little more composure than before—*that's* a step. Every time you voice your struggles instead of burying them—another step. Every honest tear that's cried and every moment you decide to keep walking forward—yet more steps. Healing is rarely flashy; it's often steady and humble, a quiet reshaping of your habits, thoughts, and reactions.

It's easy to fixate on how far you still have to go, the lingering aches that haven't disappeared. But there's power in pausing to notice the small transformations. Maybe you've learned to pause and breathe when panic arises instead of being swept away by it. Or perhaps you've started sharing your story with a trusted friend, releasing that silent weight. These modest changes might not feel earthshaking, but they prove your healing is in motion.

We often overlook incremental progress because we're waiting for that grand breakthrough: an overnight release from fear or a sudden flood of peace that never leaves. However, God often works in the quiet corners of our daily routines, teaching us to rely on Him moment by moment. Think of it as spiritual muscle-building. Day after day, you strengthen your capacity to trust, to cope, to rest in God's presence instead of anxiety's grip. A single workout doesn't transform a body; likewise, one emotional victory doesn't complete your healing. But taken together—like a series of workouts—they accumulate into a profound shift in your spirit.

Have you ever noticed how hard it can be to change a habit? Trauma, in some ways, can feel like a distorted habit your heart and mind have developed—expecting fear, bracing for danger, rehearsing worst-case scenarios. Changing that rhythm requires daily discipline. It might be starting the morning with a few minutes of silent prayer, grounding your day in God's love before doubts try to crowd in. It might look like journaling each evening, reflecting on where you felt triggered and how you responded differently than before. Slowly, these simple practices carve new neural pathways, gently teaching your brain and body that life is no longer bound by old trauma.

You expect a learning curve when learning a new skill—like playing an instrument. Mistakes happen, repetitions are needed, and patience is essential. Healing is no different. You may find yourself upset when triggers flare up again as if you've lost all the progress you made. But I urge you: show yourself grace. A setback doesn't erase the strides you've taken. Sometimes, it merely highlights where you need to focus more on care or prayer. Just as a musician practices the same chord until muscle memory takes over, you practice responding to triggers, managing anxiety, and rooting your identity in God's truth—again and again—until it becomes second nature.

If a day comes when you crumble under the weight of a painful memory or a rough trigger, don't label yourself a failure. Instead, see it as a chance to evaluate what you've learned. Maybe you need additional support, or you need to refine your coping techniques. Healing isn't a straight line; it curves, stalls, and then surges forward. Keep your eyes on the sum total of your journey rather than any single dip in the road.

One of the greatest motivators in any journey is recognizing and celebrating wins—even small ones. Maybe you got through a tense family gathering without the usual knot in your stomach. Perhaps you managed to voice a boundary when you'd have stayed silent in the past. Or you spent a night sleeping a little more peacefully than usual. Take a moment to acknowledge those milestones. Write them down, whisper a prayer of thanks, or share them with a trusted friend who can rejoice alongside you.

Celebration counters the negativity trauma often inflicts on us. It shifts your perspective from *"I'm not there yet"* to *"Look how far I've come."* It also fuels hope, reinforcing that you *can* change and that your future is not forever tied to the nightmares of the past. Over time, these small celebrations weave together into a tapestry of redemption, showing how God truly meets you in the details and leads you to a broader life.

Remember, faith is not a passive feeling; it's a decision to trust even when circumstances are uncertain. Each step forward—each new boundary, each calm breath during a trigger, each time you choose to pray instead of panic—is an act of faith. You're essentially saying, *"Lord, I may still feel the echoes of hurt, but I believe You're guiding my steps. I believe I can change."* When fear suggests you'll always be stuck, faith insists that God's power to restore is greater than any damage you've endured.

In these moments, don't underestimate the force of a simple prayer: *"Help me, God. Hold me right now."* Sometimes, that's all you can muster. And that's enough. Because healing doesn't rely on the eloquence of your words; it hinges on the sincerity of your heart and the goodness of the God who hears you. He sees each tear, each trembling fear, and longs to meet you there with comfort and courage.

Over time, these steady steps accumulate into a life that looks very different from when you first started addressing your trauma. You'll notice that the nightmares don't grip you quite as fiercely or that you bounce back more quickly when a memory resurfaces. You may find your relationships improving as you're more present and less burdened by the quiet ache that used to dominate your thoughts. This doesn't mean you'll never feel pain again. But it does mean you're learning to live from a place of hope rather than helplessness.

As you walk this path, you might suddenly realize you have enough strength to extend a hand to others who are still lost in the darkness of their wounds. Your story of incremental healing becomes a beacon for someone else who is just starting to take their own first steps. Sometimes, the greatest testament to your progress is how you can guide someone else along the way you've traveled.

So, dear friend, keep taking those daily steps. Keep breathing prayers of grace when triggers strike. Keep reflecting on how far you've come instead of focusing on the distance. Keep inviting God's love into the places where you still feel tender and raw. Healing might not happen overnight, but it's happening. You're becoming more free, grounded, and capable of seeing the horizon of a life not ruled by past trauma.

Each step is a victory. Each victory points to a faithful God who loves you enough to walk your entire journey. You are growing stronger in ways you might not fully see until you pause one day and realize the mountain you once cowered before has become a vantage point where you stand tall, breathing deeply, surveying the view of what God can do with a willing soul. So take heart—your progress is genuine, and the next step awaits you. Step by step, you're moving toward wholeness.

Reflection Questions

1. What does the phrase "healing isn't linear" mean to you after reading this chapter?

2. In moments of frustration, do you give yourself grace for where you are in the process?

3. What are small daily practices that keep you grounded in your healing journey?

4. When setbacks happen, do you see them as failures or as part of the process?

5. How can you celebrate the steps you've taken—even the messy, imperfect ones?

CHAPTER 9

SMALL VICTORIES MATTER

I magine you've been straggling through a desert, the scorching sun overhead making every step feel heavier than the last. You glance up at the horizon, longing for an oasis, yet all you see is an endless sweep of sand. It would be so easy to collapse, convinced there's no point in pressing on. But then, as you lower your gaze, you notice a single green sprout pushing through the desert floor—proof that life can thrive in hostile ground. In that tiny sprout, you see hope. That, my friend, is the power of a small victory.

When you've experienced trauma, it's normal to set your sights on grand deliverance moments—complete freedom from anxiety, an unshakeable sense of worth, or a sudden end to flashbacks. But often, the path to healing is paved with more subtle triumphs. Maybe you managed to go a whole afternoon without that sinking dread. Perhaps you spoke up for yourself in a situation where you'd usually remain silent. Or you took a few peaceful breaths during a trigger, keeping panic at bay for just another moment. These small wins might seem insignificant in the grand scheme, but let me remind you: a single green sprout in a desert can herald the presence of water just beneath the surface.

The world might overlook these mini-milestones. People celebrate big transformations and fireworks moments. But let me tell you, the God who designed you sees every effort, every careful step, every fleeting victory. Scripture reminds us not to despise "the day of small beginnings." Those small beginnings are pregnant with promise. They testify that something deeper is shifting beneath the surface of your heart, that you are indeed changing, one breath, one choice at a time.

Think about a person learning to walk again after an injury. The first time they stand on their own two feet, maybe they only manage one shaky step before needing to sit is a major accomplishment. From the outside, it might not look like much. Yet for that person, it's monumental—they've moved from dreaming about recovery to living it. The same is true for you: each time you find the courage to confront a fear, to set a boundary, or to rest in God's peace when your anxiety flares, you're taking a crucial step toward full restoration.

The beauty of celebrating small victories is that it keeps hope alive in your heart. Trauma has a way of telling you that nothing will ever improve, that you're stuck forever in a loop of pain. But when you pause to acknowledge even the tiniest progress, you break that lie. You teach your mind to recognize, *"Yes, I'm still in the process, but I'm not where I was yesterday."* There's a divine energy in that realization—it sparks gratitude, and gratitude is a powerful fuel for continued growth.

Some people shy away from celebrating minor accomplishments because they believe it's prideful or because they're afraid of getting their hopes up only to be let down. But celebrating is not about inflating your ego; it's about affirming that God is at work in you. It's about spotlighting His grace in the details of your journey. Did you handle a disagreement without spiraling into self-blame? Give thanks. Did you attend a social event without succumbing to crippling fear? Celebrate that moment. These are not random flukes; they're evidence of God's hand guiding you, and your determination partnering with that divine touch.

At times, you might wonder if you're fooling yourself, worried that small victories are overshadowed by setbacks. But remember, faith isn't about a flawless climb; it's about persevering in the face of challenge. The children of Israel took step after step across a desert, facing hunger, thirst, and enemies. Yet each time they witnessed a miracle—a manna provision, water from a rock—it was a moment of encouragement that God was still leading them forward. In your desert of healing, your small victories serve the same purpose: reminding you that you are not abandoned, that the loving presence of God is guiding you through.

And let me give you a practical tip: record these victories. Write them in a journal or note them in your phone. Maybe you keep a small jar where you drop slips of paper listing every tiny success—a day with fewer intrusive thoughts, or an instance where you replaced a negative self-accusation with a kinder truth. When you feel discouraged, pull out those records and recount each victory. Watch how your spirit lifts as you see how much your collection of small triumphs has grown. It's like building a monument to remind you, *"God brought me this far, and He will carry me further."*

Also, don't be shy about sharing these moments with someone you trust—a friend, mentor, or counselor who understands your journey. People who truly care about you will celebrate alongside you. Hearing someone say, "I'm proud of you," can strengthen your soul more than you realize. There's no shame in being affirmed; rather, it's a grace that aligns with how God cheers for each step you take away from bondage and toward wholeness.

Some days, your mind might try to dismiss small victories as trivial. That's often the trauma talking. It wants you to believe healing is impossible, so it belittles anything that doesn't look like total liberation. But the God of all creation works in seeds, not just in fully grown trees. Seeds take time to germinate. And if you constantly uproot them, complaining they're too small or too slow, you sabotage the growth that's trying to happen. So nurture those seeds of progress. Water them with gratitude, shine the light of faith upon them, and guard them from the weeds of negativity.

Picture yourself standing at the threshold of a new day. You may not yet see the entire path cleared of obstacles, but you can sense the dawn breaking. The darkness of old traumas is receding little by little. If you pay close attention, you'll notice the silhouette of small victories on the horizon, beckoning you forward. Each one you gather pushes the shadows back another inch, letting hope spill over into places that were once starved for light.

That's why small victories matter. They are the raindrops before the storm of blessing, the appetizer before the feast of deliverance, the whispered assurance before the battle's final triumph. Embrace them, celebrate them, and cling to them when your heart grows weary. They point to something bigger unfolding—a steady, God-led renewal from the inside out.

So keep your eyes open for the small progress that appears in your everyday life. Don't gloss over them in search of something grander. Grand moments have their place, but it's often in the ordinary steps, repeated faithfully, that God's extraordinary power shines brightest. And one day, you'll look back on these little wins and realize they formed a mighty foundation for the life of wholeness and purpose you were always meant to live.

Reflection Questions

1. Think back to the last time you overcame a difficult moment. Did you celebrate it or brush it aside?

2. How has perfectionism robbed you of acknowledging small but meaningful victories?

3. Why is it easier to see progress in others than it is in yourself?

4. What small win today deserves your recognition, even if it feels insignificant?

5. How does God's view of success differ from the world's? How does that change how you view your own healing?

CHAPTER 10

WHEN OLD WOUNDS STING AGAIN

T here comes a moment on every healing journey when you feel steady—like you've finally found your footing on ground that once shook beneath you. Then, out of nowhere, a reminder or a sudden memory rushes in, and it feels as though the old pain has returned to claim your peace. You might say to yourself, "I thought I was past this. Why am I hurting again?" That nudge of realization can feel defeating, even embarrassing, as if all your hard-won progress just vanished.

But listen closely: when an old wound stings again, it doesn't mean you've failed. It means you're human. Healing is rarely a neat, straight line; it's more like a winding road that leads us closer and closer to freedom with every twist and turn. Think of it as walking through a valley where the echo of your past trauma still bounces off the canyon walls. You might be further down the trail, but certain echoes—specific triggers—can still reverberate. And that's okay.

Let me paint a picture: you're going about your day, maybe enjoying a peaceful afternoon, feeling lighter than you have in a long while. Suddenly, you catch a glimpse of someone with a familiar walk, or you hear a song that once accompanied a painful chapter of your life. Instantly, your chest tightens, and your thoughts tumble back to dark corridors you'd rather forget. The wave of anxiety or sorrow hits you like a flash flood. At that moment, it's easy to believe the old lie: *"I'm right back where I started."*

But are you really? Consider all the ways you've grown. The fear might flare up again, but how quickly do you recognize it now? How soon do you remember to ground yourself, to pray, to breathe through the storm? The very fact that you're more aware and more prepared shows that healing has indeed taken root in you. Painful memories might still knock on your door, but you're learning to answer differently without giving them free rein in your heart.

A dear friend once shared with me how, after months of feeling stable, a single phone call from a toxic family member knocked the wind out of her. She sobbed that night, sure she was "broken all over again." Yet the next day, she reflected on how she responded—though it hurt, she didn't numb herself like she used to. She reached out to her support system, prayed through her fears, and journaled her emotions. It wasn't easy, but she discovered a new resilience in herself. That's the subtle but very real progress we often overlook in moments of crisis.

There's a story in the Scriptures about Elijah, a mighty prophet who stood boldly against false prophets on Mount Carmel. He witnessed a tremendous victory of God's power. But right after that breakthrough, he spiraled into despair when threatened by Jezebel. He fled into the wilderness, convinced he was alone and unsafe, even asking God to take his life. How could someone so strong in faith be reduced to trembling fear? Because old wounds, lingering exhaustion, and real terror can stir up even after a triumph. Yet in that valley of despair, God met Elijah gently, providing rest, nourishment, and a renewed sense of purpose. Likewise, you can hold both victory and vulnerability in the same hands, and God will meet you there, too.

So, what do you do when those old wounds sting again? First, recognize it for what it is: a *setback*, not the end of your healing. Second, ground yourself—maybe close your eyes and take several slow, deliberate breaths. Remind your mind and body, *"I'm safe right now. This is a reminder of pain, not a new betrayal."* Whisper a prayer: *"Lord, I feel fear, but I trust You hold me in this moment."* That small act of faith can stop old trauma from flooding your entire sense of being. Third, look at what triggered this sting. Did a particular event, sight, or smell spark the memory? Understanding the cause can help you handle or avoid similar triggers in the future—or at least be prepared when they arise.

Don't be afraid to talk it through. Whether you call a trusted friend, reach out to a pastor, or journal your thoughts, putting words to the experience helps you see it more objectively. You realize it isn't an unstoppable force taking over your life; it's an echo—loud, yes, but still just an echo of a pain you've already confronted. And if you find yourself needing more support again—a counselor or a trauma-focused group—it's not a weakness to seek that help. It's wisdom. Even the strongest among us need refreshing or re-centering when the battle rears its head once more.

One more thing: pray for patience with yourself. We live in a world that idolizes instant fixes. But heart-level healing is more like planting seeds in a field once scorched by fire. The new growth emerges tenderly. Some plants might get trampled or wither under a hot sun, but we keep tending them. Over time, that field grows greener, the roots go deeper, and soon enough, you have a flourishing garden where only ash and ruin stood before. Your own heart, in God's loving care, can do the same.

So if an old wound stings again, treat it like a passing storm. Storms can rattle the windows and make you anxious, but they pass. And if your foundation is built on truth, prayer, and the progress you've worked so hard to cultivate, you'll stand even if the wind howls. You may come out the other side with a couple of new branches broken off and a fresh bruise on your spirit, but you'll still be standing. And that, dear friend, is a testament to how far you've journeyed.

In that moment, you'll remember: healing isn't a final destination you arrive at once and for all; it's a living, evolving process. Some days, you feel unstoppable; others, you feel fragile. Through it all, God's unwavering presence, your learned resilience, and the new skills you've gained combine to keep you moving forward. So the next time an old wound flares up, whisper to your heart, *"This pain is real, but it's not forever. I am stronger than I was. My scars tell a story of survival, not defeat."*

Yes, the sting may return now and then, but so will the triumph. You have the tools, the faith, and the community of support to walk through any dark valley. Each time you do, you'll discover another layer of strength—another testament to the truth that even old wounds can't stop a soul determined to heal and a God faithful to redeem.

Reflection Questions

1. When old pain resurfaces, what's your first emotional reaction? Do you push it away, or sit with it?

2. How have you handled seasons when it felt like you were "back at square one" in your healing journey?

3. What patterns keep you stuck in cycles of pain, and what's one step toward breaking them?

4. How does God's grace cover you even in moments of relapse, doubt, or emotional spirals?

5. What would it look like to extend the same patience and compassion to yourself that God offers you?

CHAPTER 11

EMBRACING YOUR STORY

Think back to the moments in your life that shaped you—both the beautiful and the brutal. There might have been instances so joyous they made your heart soar and others so painful you doubted you'd ever rise again. Trauma lingers in that painful territory, convincing you it's the sole author of your narrative. But what if I told you that your story is more than the wounds you've endured, that the shadows of your past don't get the final say?

The world often measures us by the shiniest parts of our lives—our successes, our polished presentations. Meanwhile, we hide the bruised chapters, hoping no one will see the flaws. Yet, every page of your story matters in the kingdom of God. Every chapter. Every scar. Every tear. They're wool knitted to create the perfect sweater and become more intricate than you could imagine. And the astonishing truth is that no matter how dark some of those yarns are, the shirt can become vividly colorful and captivating because of its patterns.

When you've faced trauma, it's easy to think, *"I'm ruined. My story is just too broken."* But do you realize that in Scripture, God has a habit of taking people with wounded backgrounds and turning them into vessels of grace? Look at Joseph, who endured betrayal and wrongful imprisonment, only to later say, *"You meant evil against me, but God meant it for good."* Or consider Ruth an outsider and a widow whose faithfulness led her into the lineage of kings. Their most challenging chapters weren't erased; they were redeemed. And if God did it for them, He can do it for you.

This chapter is about coming to terms with your own story and scars while embracing every layer, every lesson, and every trace of hope that still flickers beneath the surface. Maybe you've spent years wishing you could tear out certain pages and bury them so deep that memory can't find them. But part of the healing process is learning to say, *"Yes, that happened, but it does not define the totality of who I am."* Trauma might have shaped certain aspects of your journey. But there's a deeper identity within you that can't be destroyed by any tragedy or betrayal.

Think of your life as a book that has plenty of chapters. Some chapters might be heart-wrenching, and you recoil at the mere thought of re-reading them. Other chapters might be filled with triumphs or laughter so pure you want to bottle it. Collectively, they form the narrative of you—a narrative still being written. Embracing your story means you don't skip over the painful parts, but you also don't let them overshadow the rest. You acknowledge their impact and glean whatever wisdom or empathy they can yield. Still, you keep turning pages, anticipating what new plot twists grace might usher in.

For the longest time, you might have allowed shame to silence you. But naming your past isn't about glorifying the hurt or wallowing in self-pity. It's about releasing the grip shame has on your heart. When you dare to say, *"This happened, and I survived,"* you snatch away the power that secrecy once held. You begin to realize that you are more than a victim; you are, in fact, a survivor—a living testimony that darkness didn't prevail.

Embracing your story also invites you into deeper compassion for yourself. It's recognizing that the person you were back then did the best they could with the resources and knowledge they had. In hindsight, we all see what we *could have* done better, but you didn't have that foresight then. So be kind to yourself. Accept that the version of you who went through those trials deserves understanding, not judgment. Often, self-compassion is the first step toward dismantling guilt, regret, or harsh self-criticism.

And oh, the freedom that comes when you no longer feel the need to hide. It doesn't mean you parade every detail of your trauma in public. Instead, you walk through life unafraid of being "found out" because you've owned your story. You've stared your hurts in the face, called them by name, and invited God's redemptive love into every crevice. So, if someone asks about your past or comments on your scars, you no longer flinch. You can acknowledge them with honesty—perhaps even gratitude for the strength you discovered along the way.

Embracing your story offers you the chance to be a beacon for others. Picture how comforting it is when you meet a person who has walked the same rocky road and lived to tell the tale. Their presence alone can breathe life into your weary bones because you see living proof that the valley has an exit. Now imagine that *you* could be that person for someone else. Your story, once cloaked in shame, might become the key that unlocks hope in another heart. You might speak or write a single sentence that resonates with someone who thought they were beyond help. That's the beauty of redemption: what was once a source of anguish becomes a wellspring of compassion and connection.

Of course, it takes discernment. You may share your story in bits and pieces. Not everyone is equipped to hold it with care. But when you find that friend, counselor, or community that honors your vulnerability, your willingness to tell the truth of your journey can ignite transformation—not just in you, but in them, too. Because truth spoken in love breaks chains on multiple levels.

If you still fear seeing yourself as "tainted" or "ruined," hear me now: You are not the worst thing that's happened to you. You are not the darkest night you endured. The divine image stamped on your soul cannot be erased by trauma. Yes, pain leaves a mark, but so does the refining fire of resilience. God can breathe purpose into your experiences, showing you new ways to serve, new paths to empathy, and a new capacity to love deeper and brighter than before.

So, dear friend, step into the light with your story in hand. Remember the times you stumbled, the lessons you gleaned, and the persistent hope that refused to die within you. Embracing your story doesn't mean you celebrate the evil done to you or gloss over the heartbreak—it means you stand tall in the conviction that not a single chapter will be wasted. You're a survivor with a future, not merely a victim with a past.

As you carry this perspective, let your heart rest in the knowledge that each scar can be a signpost pointing to deliverance. Each chapter of pain is also a chapter of perseverance. And in God's hands, your story becomes a living parable, whispering to the world that joy can triumph over sorrow, that faith can outlast fear, and that resurrection can follow even the bleakest crucifixion moments.

Yes, the time has come to embrace your story fully. Don't hide from it, don't dismiss it. Claim it as yours—not as an anchor to sink you, but as a testament to the saving grace that has sustained you up to this point. In doing so, you not only honor the person you once were; you lift your eyes to the expansive horizon God has set before you. Because the best part of your story is still unfolding, and I promise you, it's worth every page.

Reflection Questions

1. If you had to sum up your story in one sentence, what would it say right now? What do you want it to say a year from now?

2. What parts of your story still carry shame? How can you start seeing them through the lens of grace?

3. Imagine sharing your story with someone who needs hope. What would you want them to hear most?

4. How has your definition of strength changed after walking through trauma and healing?

5. What would it look like for you to stop surviving and start thriving?

Epilogue

You've traveled a road few dare to openly speak of—the road of scars and the struggles they represent. Yet look at you now, standing closer to the light, having dared to gaze upon wounds you once hid in the shadows. With each chapter, you chose to let honesty guide you deeper into truths about your body, your mind, and your heart. You might feel tender still, like a fresh bandage covers old stitches, but do not mistake tenderness for weakness. It's a sign of new life emerging where pain tried to claim the final word.

Scars once whispered that you were defined by what happened to you, but in these pages, you found a different story. You discovered that your scars mark survival, not defeat. You faced triggers, recognized the silent weight of shame, and dared to speak aloud the hurts that had festered in silence. You noticed how God's steady hand, like a beacon, can guide you even on days when you stumble. And when the old wound stung once more, you refused to bow to despair. Each step proved that "Scarred" doesn't mean "stuck"; it's merely evidence that you've endured, and by grace, you're still rising.

As you close this book, remember that healing is not a finish line. It's a journey—one you'll continue. There may be moments when memories try to pull you backward. But you have tools now, revelation and faith that remind you darkness isn't eternal. You've learned to honor small victories, embrace each step forward, and stand tall in your story rather than shrink from it. Those scars that once tormented you can become symbols of God's power to redeem, testifying to the resilience He placed within you from the very start.

If you find yourself unsure at times—wondering if you can truly live beyond the echo of old trauma—take a breath and recall how far you've come. Pray, reflect, and reach out to those who can stand with you. Lean on the voice of faith that whispers hope into every weary sigh. Even in moments when you feel a setback looming, do not let fear convince you your progress was all for nothing. Each new day offers a fresh chance to grow stronger, to trust deeper, and to flourish like never before.

This is not goodbye; it's an invitation to keep becoming. Your scars testify that life tried to break you, but it couldn't. They show that with every wound, a divine hand can bring healing, purpose, and strength beyond measure. Carry that hope with you, letting it shape your to-morrows. And if ever you need a reminder of how brave you are, trace your scars with gentle hands and remember the love of the One who walks beside you, rewriting every chapter of your story with grace.

Go forward in faith, renewed by the promise that you are whole and held. Your journey is far from over, but it's brimming with the potential of a life not defined by scars but liberated through them. May you walk boldly into the future, knowing that who you are becoming holds far more power than what you've endured. Let your scars point to the God who redeems, and never forget—you are not alone, you are not defined by the past, and you are cherished more than words can say.

What's Next

Take a moment to breathe. You've navigated the terrain of *Scarred*, shining a compassionate light on those hidden aches you once tucked away. It can be overwhelming—confronting the depth of past hurts, learning to speak honestly about what haunted your midnight hours. Yet here you stand, on the other side of these pages, having named your pains and gained clarity. It's an act of courage few dare, and you've done it with grace.

Now, you might be asking, *"Where do I go from here?"* The next stage in **The Trauma Detox** series is *Mended*. If *Scarred* was the unveiling of truth—acknowledging the weight of your wounds—*Mended* becomes the daily regimen of gentle practices that help mend those wounds over time. In *Mended*, you'll discover faith-rooted exercises, tips to form new rhythms of calm, and practical steps to rebuild trust in relationships. The routines you build and the small victories you notice will create a foundation of stability that trauma once denied you.

But before you leap into *Mended*, pause to honor the progress already made. You dared to speak what once felt unspeakable. You invited God into the silent corners of your memory, allowing a glimmer of hope to seep in. Take a day, a week, or however long you need to breathe, pray, and let the seeds of self-awareness settle. Jot down any reflections or breakthroughs you want to carry forward—moments when you felt a rush of relief or times you sensed that the Holy Spirit was gently nudging you toward freedom.

Only then proceed to *Mended* at your own pace. You'll find it an active guide: a companion that translates the revelations of *Scarred* into daily life patterns. Think of it as moving from recognition to reconstruction, from identification of pain to implementing tangible strategies that lighten its load. Let your heart remain open as you continue, trusting that the One who guided you through *Scarred* stands ready to shepherd you through the next leg of this healing expedition.

Above all, keep reminding yourself that your past does not have the final say. You've declared, "I have scars, but they do not define me." The choice now is to pursue the next steps with faith and expectation. Each page of *Mended* will reaffirm that old wounds can indeed mend, layering hope upon every bruise. So gather your courage, hold fast to the insights you've gained, and step forward, knowing that you are on the road to a life far better and freer than trauma ever wanted you to believe. Your journey, dear friend, is not ending here—it's reaching upward to the next summit of wholeness.

THE END

www.ingramcontent.com/pod-product-compliance
Lightning Source LLC
Chambersburg PA
CBHW072202090426
42740CB00012B/2360